Victoria

Romantic Window Style

Victoria

Romantic Window Style

ALEXANDRA PARSONS

HEARST BOOKS
A Division of Sterling Publishing Co., Inc.
New York

Library of Congress Cataloging-in-Publication Data

Parsons, Alexandra.
    Victoria romantic window style / Alexandra Parsons.
        p.cm.
    Includes index.
    ISBN 1-58816-308-3
      1. Windows in interior decoration. 2. Draperies in inerior
decoration. 3. Victoriana in
  interior decoration. I. Title.

NK2121.P37 2004
747'.5--dc22   2003057098

10 9 8 7 6 5 4 3 2 1

Published by Hearst Books
A Division of Sterling Publishing Co., Inc.
387 Park Avenue South, New York, N.Y. 10016

        Hearst Books is proud to continue the superb style, quality,
and tradition of *Victoria* magazine with every book we publish. On our
beautifully illustrated pages you will always find inspiration and ideas about the
subjects you love.

Victoria is a trademark owned by Hearst Magazines Property, Inc.,
in USA, and Hearst Communications, Inc., in Canada.
Hearst Books is a trademark owned by Hearst Communications, Inc.

Distributed in Canada by Sterling Publishing
c/o Canadian Manda Group, One Atlantic Avenue, Suite 105
Toronto, Ontario, Canada M6K 3E7

Distributed in Australia by Capricorn Link (Australia) Pty. Ltd.
P.O. Box 704, Windsor, NSW 2756 Australia

Printed in China

ISBN 1-58816-308-3
Designed by Christine Wood

Contents

Introduction

It is difficult to imagine a room without fabrics because they give a room such atmosphere. And, there is no better way to enjoy fabrics than to hang them at a window as the focal point of any room. There can be no doubt that the window treatments you choose for your home will have a tremendous impact on its ambiance and define your style—whether your preference is for mere wisps of sheer organza, the lean lines of slatted blinds, or the dramatic elegance of full, formal curtains.

Interior designers like to start looking at a room with an eye for its architecture, and because windows are an essential part of that, they consider the walls and window treatments at the same time. If major renovations are to be done, designers will make sure to accommodate curtain or blind headings and hardware, because they know that the room will not work well if the windows and the window treatments have not been thought through carefully from the very beginning.

Because curtains do make an impression, it is easy to know where to start if you want to give your room a significant makeover. By changing your curtains, swapping curtains for blinds, or doing something as minor as adding a new colorful braid or a beaded tieback to existing curtains, you can wake up an entire décor and give your room a whole new focus.

CHAPTER ONE

Working with the Architecture

Curtains offer a wonderful opportunity to soften the lines of a room, add color and warmth, emphasize good proportions, and improve on bad ones. Your first consideration when choosing a style of curtain should be to work with the architecture of the room.

Curtains with a swagger and a sense of humor. A stunning room in which the curtains make a statement way beyond expectations for a classical Georgian interior. Multiple layers of fabric are tied back and twisted to show off their underskirts in a postmodern take on the traditional swag and tail.

Appropriate treatments

Your choice of window treatment will depend as much on the style of the interior architecture as on your personal decorative style. A grand room with elegant Palladian proportions, for instance, will require an entirely different approach than a modern glass extension. Curtains are a tool to help you achieve the atmosphere you want, and they should be right at the top of the list of decisions, along with the color of the walls—not an afterthought like a scatter cushion.

Let the room inspire you: a country bedroom with French windows opening onto a meadow would suggest a light, unstructured treatment of gauzy linens billowing in the breeze, while a smart dining room used only at night is an opportunity to indulge in a rich swath of jewel-colored silk, lined and interlined, spilling heavily to the floor.

Opposite page: Full-length brocade curtains hang like fluted pillars at either side of these elegant, multipaned windows. The artfully shaped and tasseled pelmet draws attention to the curves of the arches. It is fixed under a wooden cornice that echoes the shape of a classical pediment.

Below: In a rustic log cabin with pitch pine walls, a translucent muslin curtain lies in bunches casually on the windowsill.

The warm wood paneling in this Colonial-style room is enhanced by the muted colors and elegant style of the curtain treatments. The curtain pole is part of the architecture of the window frame.

Tobacco-colored silk drapes soften the lines of the windows and draw the eye up to the ceiling. The softly pleated swag is perfectly in keeping with the gracious ambiance of this room.

A soft silk fringe on the leading edge of the asymmetrical drapes emphasizes the rippling line of the pleats.

These deep-set windows finish with a broad windowsill, and wooden Colonial shutters are the perfect solution for providing privacy and controlling light.

Emphasize the vertical

Tall, narrow windows are the easiest to dress, and their elegant proportions give a room height and grandeur. Use curtain treatments to emphasize the vertical elements of a room, leaving the horizontal plane to the furniture.

Height can be achieved by illusion, by giving visual interest to the top of the window in the form of an interesting heading such as a restrained swag or by using a boldly striped fabric to draw the eye upward. Curtains should extend from the ceiling even if the window itself stops short at a windowsill, and they should fall to the floor, touching it by just less than an inch.

Right: Dining rooms are generally nighttime rooms. Here, full-length curtains enclose diners in an inviting environment with a welcome splash of warm color. The stripes emphasize the vertical plane, drawing the eye upward to the pièce de résistance—a crystal chandelier.

Pelmets and valances can be the crowning glory of a formal curtain treatment, and they certainly carry the eye upward. For a very tall window in a high-ceilinged room, adding a pelmet of some kind is a good visual trick for making the room seem more intimate by lowering the top of the window.

On the plus side, pelmets hide all evidence of tracks and fitting mechanisms. On the negative side, formal, shaped pelmets look old-fashioned and they do cut out light.

Pelmets should be thought of as fitting in with the architecture of the cornice; thus, they work best on tall windows that go right up to the ceiling and with full-length curtains. In contrast, they look busy on squat, horizontal windows. The more modern style of soft, unstructured valances or a simple swag looped over a pole fits in well with relaxed, informal interiors.

Opposite page: A gently curving pelmet echoes the curve of the large bay window.

Right: The casual curves of the softly draped valance make the windows less angular and add interest to the tops of tall windows.

Cosmetic surgery

For rooms with less than perfect proportions, curtains perform instant cosmetic surgery. In rooms that have been carved out of larger spaces— for instance, loft conversions or grand houses partitioned into new apartments—the windows are often oddly shaped, asymmetrical, or in the wrong place. However, a warehouse window cut brutally in half by a mezzanine floor could be made to look like part of the architecture with a softening swath of fabric where the top of the window should have been. A window that is set off to one side—perhaps the most difficult of all to deal with—can be disguised by balancing it with a fake set of curtains at the other end of the wall.

Left: A pair of lined and interlined thick silk curtains act as a room divider, giving the colorful dining area under the mezzanine level its own identity.

Above: A French window with glorious views is framed by long, relaxed curtains in unlined silk.

Facing page: The top half of a magnificent arched window in a converted church. The tied-back curtains add soft curves of their own.

Exploit the cosmetic effect of curtains to enhance a beautiful window or to accentuate that long, lean style that makes a room look so elegant. Classical architects didn't just use pillars to prop things up, they used them because they lead the eye upward—and that is what a column of fabric on either side of a window can do.

The primary function of a window is to let in light and air during the day. Curtains and blinds affect the way sunlight streams into the room and the way shadows fall by masking views or enhancing them. And this is why window treatments make such a fundamental difference: essentially, they are the interface between the room and the outside world.

Accentuate the positive

- Hang curtains as close to the ceiling as possible but leave them long enough to graze the floor.

- Let curtains work with the architecture of your room, not against it. If your windows have magnificent surroundings, do not hide them.

- In rooms where complete dark is unnecessary, use sheer, translucent curtains to provide privacy while letting in light.

- Use curtains and blinds as cosmetic surgery to emphasize good points and to detract from architectural flaws.

- Pelmets and valances, if used, should not be too long since the light that comes in from the top of a window is the brightest.

Working with the window

The shape and type of your window will often suggest a treatment, and while curtain makers follow certain general rules, it is often in breaking them that the most startling effects emerge.

Tall, narrow windows give a room elegance and grandeur, and the best thing you can do with these is simply to hang floor-to-ceiling curtains. Avoid overdressing such windows, because doing so detracts from their perfect proportions.

French windows that open inward require wall space on either side so that curtains stay well out of the way. French windows look better without pelmets or valances, which act as visual barriers.

Deep-set windows look their best with blinds or shutters covering the actual window area and dress curtains, if necessary, hanging to the side.

Left: These beautifully arched French windows open outward. Their generous width makes them the perfect candidate for this striking treatment. Unlined silk has been gathered up, or ruched, onto a curved pole, and the curtains are held well clear of the window with a cord that pulls the curtains up and open in the same dramatic way as a theater curtain.

Bay windows are the most difficult to deal with because of all the tracks and hardware that have to be set just above the window. If you deal with the bay window in sections, you have bunches of fabric hanging within the alcove. One solution is to have pulling curtains on either side that obliterate the window when drawn; another is to use lightweight curtains to cover the actual window and dress curtains on either side.

Tall, narrow, arched windows are generally dealt with by ignoring the arch and hanging curtains up to the ceiling on either side, making sure that the line of the arch is visible when the curtains are open. Wide arches, on the other hand, are prime candidates for imaginative headings that follow their gentle curves.

Left: A shallow bay window in a pretty, pastel bedroom. The full-length curtains give the bay window a feeling of grandeur, while the delicate scalloped valance softens the top. The whole treatment beautifully blends in with the walls and the overall design.

Opposite page: A window built into a recess deep enough to house a cozy cushioned window seat. Dress curtains to either side frame the recess, while a ruched blind hangs atop the window itself, controlling light and ensuring privacy.

The long and the short

● Use full-length dress curtains to frame bay windows and recesses. Because dress curtains are not made to be pulled, they can be arranged in elegant pleats and folds and gathered into interesting tiebacks.

● Use blinds or shutters on deep-set windows. They are easier to reach and operate than curtains and they stay clear of the window area, letting in the light.

● Formal dress curtains should be lined and interlined and weighted at the bottom.

● French windows that open into the room need sufficient wall space on either side of the window to store the curtains.

● French windows that open outward should have curtains that tie back, out of the way.

Most homes possess at least one awkward window—a skylight, clerestory, or dormer that was probably added at a later stage to admit light or air. If they need to be covered for the sake of privacy or to keep out light, then custom-made blinds or shutters are the neatest solution.

Walls of glass present another dilemma. If they look good, privacy isn't a concern, and the view beyond is wonderful, then leave them alone. There can be a problem at night, however, when that sparkling wall of glass turns into a black hole. One solution is to illuminate the view outside; another is to install sliding panels of fabric or a free-standing screen.

Left: A neat solution for an attic bedroom with an unsightly dormer. Fabric has been stretched over ceiling and walls and into the recesses of the deep-set dormer window. The matching curtains have been secured at the top by the central beam and at their bottom edge by a rail concealed in the angle where walls meet the sloping ceiling. The result is a stylish tentlike effect.

Glazing bars are a feature that can be played up. They have a pleasing architectural rhythm and cast interesting shadows into the room.

The window is the most dominant aspect of this dining room. With a beautiful view of the garden, and such elegantly proportioned windows, curtains are unneccessary. The frames themselves become part of the window dressing.

This room is all about symmetry, which has been emphasized by placing matching urns either side of the window.

Working with the walls

Curtain fabric is not something that can be chosen in isolation. It has to be part of a decorative whole. In historic houses with ornate cornicing and plasterwork, curtain fabrics and pelmet details were carefully considered and curtain treatments were practically built into the room. They were often designed by the original architect and were expected to last for generations.

In modern homes, blending window treatments with the wall is an excellent way to emphasize space. Avoid a slavish match of wallpaper and fabric because it now looks distinctly old-fashioned and can feel quite overwhelming from within. What is preferable is a subtle blending so that walls and curtain treatments work in harmony with one another.

Opposite page: Mixing and nearly matching. The subtle patterns on the white-on-white wallpaper are picked up by these simple cotton muslin curtains that display a similar cutout design on a larger scale.

Left: Perfect harmony. In a magnificent historic home, the ornate cornicing and border on the walls is echoed in the wonderful sweep of the silk velvet pelmet. Reds and golds glow harmoniously, and patterns echo patterns.

Blending in

- Consider wall treatments and curtains at the same time. If they work well together, the room will benefit.

- An interesting way to use the same fabric on both walls and windows is to reverse it on the walls, so that it looks the same yet subtly different.

- Modern rooms, where space and the feeling of space are vital, look best with the simplest of wall/window treatments: that is, white walls with white blinds.

- Give rooms used mainly at night, such as a dining room, a dramatic and womb-like look with integrated wall/window schemes in bright colors.

- Hide ugly or strangely positioned windows with a matching wall/window design.

Interior designers often gather swatches of fabric and trimmings, paint colors, and flooring samples and play around with them until a theme becomes apparent. This is a tried-and-tested way of coming up with the bones of a decorative design that works. Then they have to decide how much of what goes where.

It is very easy to be seduced by a strongly patterned fabric that you love. Of course, using yards and yards of it at the window would give it the greatest impact—but less is often more in interior design terms, and a wonderful fabric might suit the room better if used as a trimming for a curtain, as a blind, or as a cushion cover.

Right: A riot of color in a beautifully proportioned room. It is hard to go wrong with proportions like these. Bold, colorful stripes on fabric stretched on the walls and simply pleated at the window make this study bright and inviting by day and dramatically tentlike by night.

Opposite page: A perfect match. This monochrome bedroom uses the same fabrics on the walls as at the window.

Color is one way to encourage walls and curtains to blend harmoniously; pattern is another, with maybe a shift in scale or color of the pattern to add interest; another approach is to use texture. The soft sheen of a silk-finish paint, for example, can be picked up in a silky fabric or contrasted with a nubbly linen or a coarsely woven wool.

Fabric technology has advanced so much in the last ten years that it is now possible to have fabrics and wall coverings made of metal, leather, rubber, or suede, and for the adventurous, endless possibilities exist. If your tastes tend more to the conventional, then fabric technology has freed you as well. It is now possible to have unlined silk curtains billowing at your window without fear of sun damage or rot setting in.

Left: A relaxing space with subtle textures. Unlined gray-blue silk dress curtains hang simply from a pinch-pleat heading on either side of a French window. Unlined white undercurtains pick up the soft white of the walls.

The no-curtain solution

The purpose of curtains is to block out light and provide privacy. In days gone by, thick curtains were a first line of defense against bitter drafts from ill-fitting casements. Now that we enjoy double glazing and central heating, there is one less reason for having curtains everywhere.

Some rooms do need curtains, and not just for practical reasons. They need them for the general ambiance, the dampening of sound, and the feeling of warmth and comfort that they bring. However, some rooms and some windows are best left unadorned.

Below left: Curtains and kitchens do not mix well, and where there is no privacy issue, there's no need—especially when the windows are as attractive as this pair.

It would be such a shame to hide this stunning view, and these full-height windows really let in the light. As privacy is not an issue in this house, the architect has made the most of the double-height room.

Dramatic windows like these are a feature in their own right — the frames form an impressive grid pattern that helps to break up the huge window.

Stripped, wooden floors complete the clean, modern look, and help to reflect even more light around the room.

The no-curtain choice requires some courage, and it is not advisable unless you have a good view. If you do enjoy a fabulous view, then think of your window frame as the enclosing artwork and resist the temptation to decorate for decoration's sake.

Traditional Georgian windows had wooden shutters set into the reveals, obviating the need for curtains that might otherwise obscure the beautiful architraving of the frame. A concealed blind or external wooden shutters would be today's equivalent of that look. Sometimes a room does need a swath of fabric to soften its appearance, but there's no reason for curtains to hang at windows—instead, try them in doorways or as room dividers.

Left: A sash window frames a lovely view of a private garden. Plants and vases of cut flowers make wonderful diffusers of light.

Enjoying the view

● If you have a fabulous view and a well-proportioned window, enjoy them. Don't clutter the window with curtains. If the expanse of glass looks like a black hole at night, then light up the garden.

● Some shapes, like round windows, defy curtains. Think of using colored or tinted glass instead.

● If privacy is paramount, use concealed blinds or even electrically activated glass that becomes dark at the flick of a switch.

Below: A cheerful striped awning controls the sunlight flooding into this relaxed white-on-white living and dining room.

● You can soften the view from within and without with strategically placed plants.

● If you want the impact of fabric, use curtains in unexpected places—instead of a door, for instance.

CHAPTER TWO

Simple Style

Simple white muslin curtains billowing in the wind are the epitome
of an unstructured, attractive, and easygoing style. If patterns are used,
they come in checks, plaids, or simple floral prints, and the color palette
is neutral and soft.

*A country bedroom with a romantic touch achieved by hanging ready-made voile
curtains from poles above the beds.*

Plain & simple

Plain white curtains and walls are very appealing: an all-white look gives a room a wonderfully restful neutral base and concentrates the eye on shape and shadow. Working with plain fabric is an opportunity to explore texture—from the translucence of muslin or cotton voile to the crispness of cotton lace and the thick texture of heavy linen. The way you want your curtains to hang will dictate the weight of the fabric you choose. Heavy fabrics hold pleats and folds while the lightweight ones shift and shimmer.

To add interest to an all-white curtain treatment, try mixing textures, with a pair of smart linen dress curtains falling in columns either side of the window and a blind made from a translucent self-patterned voile or a length of delicate lace.

Right: Fine linen curtains filter light into the room and form a backdrop to a pretty lamp with a shade decorated with crystal drops. Glass looks good positioned in front of a window where light can dance through it.

Far right: The simplest way to achieve the romantic four-poster look is to slot pairs of curtains onto a pole affixed to the ceiling. There is a good contrast of textures here, with the plain cotton drapes, the crisp lace edging, and the textured bed cover.

You can do amazing things with simple materials. For a start, they are far less expensive than chintzes and brocades, so you can use great volumes of fabric, which always looks good.

If you intend to use ready-made curtains, which are perfect for this simple look, then double them up, since they are made from one width of fabric, which usually looks too skimpy. Try mixing the colors—blues and whites for a cool seaside look, pinks and oranges for a warm exotic glow. Ready-mades usually come with loop headings, which look neat, or tie headings, which look more informal. They can be threaded onto rustic wooden poles, sleek metal ones, or even lengths of bamboo or twigs.

Left: A white café curtain with a slot heading is threaded onto a simple pole, ensuring privacy from prying eyes while letting in the light. The best quality of light comes from the top of a window.

Right: A trio of pretty fabrics adorns a bedroom window seat. The tailored and buttoned cushion is made from a crisp fine linen, a length of embroidered voile hangs at the window, and a lovely piece of faded rose-print cotton covers the sill.

Left: Plain doesn't have to mean white. These cheerful yellow curtains let in the light and add a warm glow to the room.

Right page: A gorgeous billow of blue surrounds the bed, and ethereal curtains at the window give this room a hint of fairytale romance.

Plain and pretty

● Solid, neutral-colored fabrics at the window concentrate the eye on the architecture.

● Blocks of solid color at the windows suffuse a room with atmosphere.

● A monochrome design is a wonderful opportunity to mix and match textures.

● Unlined curtains have a fluidity about them that is simple and modern.

● Instead of lining curtains, try using several layers.

● New fabric technology means that treated fabrics will not disintegrate or discolor in the sun.

● Making a border in a different fabric completely alters the look of a curtain. It may be all you need do to revamp your curtains and give a room a new look.

Simple country

The simple country look embraces a whole range of styles. The relaxed Cape Cod beach house look has its collections of driftwood, its whitewashed clapboards, wooden shutters, and faded touches of sea-spray blues, greens, and grays. The French country look, popular everywhere, is epitomized by warm terra-cotta tiles, colored plaster walls, printed linens and cottons, and elegant touches of Louis XIV style. English Country style tends to resemble the slightly eccentric faded formality of the Edwardian country house, which at first suggests yards of chintz and old gold braid, but even within this style, a simple approach to window treatments can look stunning.

Country-style fabrics should be natural and casual—linens, cottons, and wools rather than shiny synthetics or gilded brocades. Country-style patterns evoke the outdoors, and pretty floral prints and embroidery or crisp ginghams are reminiscent of a tablecloth thrown down in a meadow in anticipation of a summer picnic.

Above: This window is unencumbered by curtains. The sunlight filters through a vintage embroidered blouse and onto a vase crammed with pale pink peonies.

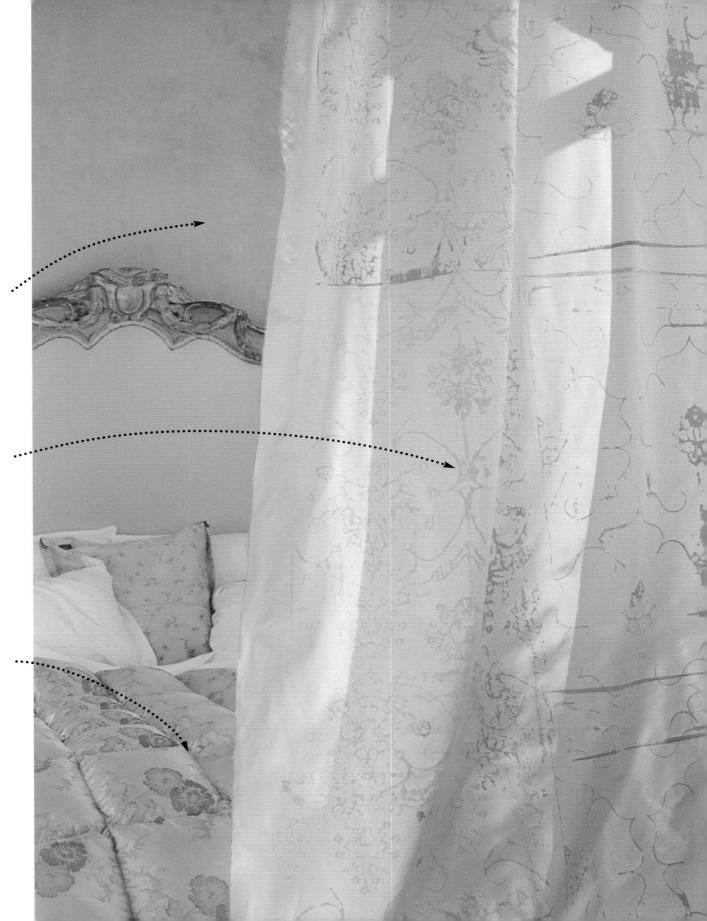

This room is very French country with its elegant upholstered and gilded bedstead and the subtle rose pigment on the distressed plaster walls.

The faded pattern on this bed curtain depicts finely etched blooms. The faint hint of color picks up the rosy walls and quilt and the dull gold of the carved headboard.

This rose quilt is patterned with darker tones of the same color, adding a strong note of color.

Opposite page: A modern take on country chic. The traditional-style, floral-patterned chairs are complemented by a pretty plain fabric at the windows.

Right: A simple bathroom with traditional fittings and white-painted tongue-and-groove boarding on the walls has plenty of rustic character. The room gets a touch of warmth and a sense of privacy thanks to a sheer checkered café curtain hung across the window frame on a wire.

Country patterns

- The way to combine floral prints with geometric stripes or checks is to match their colors.

- Pattern on pattern is very much a country look: When it works, it looks great.

- Bring the impact of your curtains into the rest of the room by reprising the color in a cushion or a throw.

- Simple checkered linings look wonderful on solid-colored or white curtains, and they present a cheerful face to the outside world.

- Mix patterns on curtains by adding hems or borders in a coordinating pattern. Borders should not go all around the curtain, just the hem and the leading edge; otherwise they look very odd.

Left: Big bold checks at the window cannot be ignored, especially when the tablecloth shares the same design on a smaller scale. Playing with the scale of patterns is a good way to add interest to an interior design.

Opposite page, left: A clever mix of pattern on pattern (all-over pattern). The reds and creams of the furnishing fabric and the curtains are enlivened with a jolt of bright pink from the chintz cushion covers.

Opposite page, right: Cotton plaid has a casual, fresh feel to it. Investigate inexpensive and cheerful mattress tickings for an interesting range of stripes and checks.

Country colors are as varied as blooms in the flower bed, but avoid changing palettes completely from room to room. A comfortable, easy-living home is one with a theme running through it, so that the view from one room to another is harmonious.

Curtains are a wonderful way to achieve a sense of unity. For instance, if you were to choose a red-and-cream floral print for the living room, you could have the same fabric in solid cream in the room leading from it, or maybe a blind in the floral print under dress curtains in one of the solid colors.

Curtain styles are another way to unite spaces. Keep to the same basic shape, adding and subtracting elements like valances and tiebacks according to the formality of the room.

Left: A log cabin with attitude and a chandelier. A curtain in a muted William Morris–type design is lined in cream and tied back with a simple rope: very elegant, very simple.

Opposite page, left: Painted plants and lilac walls. Both the curtain and the wall hanging bring a breezy, outdoor touch to this relaxing bedroom.

Opposite page, right: Floral curtains blowing in the breeze. Curtains at French windows should have room to be drawn well back on either side, well out of the way of the opening window.

Bringing the outdoors in is one of the joys of decorating country style, and the window is in the front line. You do not want to obscure views, light, or fresh air with heavy, inappropriate treatments such as deep pelmets that cut out light, or complex draperies and blinds that get in the way of the window being flung open. Pretty floral patterns, or plain greens and creams complement houseplants and bring into the home an echo of the garden beyond.

Simple sheers

Wonderful things have been happening in the field of fabric technology recently, and nowhere is this trend more evident than in the manufacture of sheer, transparent fabrics. These new sheers will not disintegrate, fade, or tear; they can be acid-etched, have designs stamped into them, and carry the weight of heavy embroidery without sagging or puckering. Some have leaves or beads sewn into them, some are woven with two different colors, and, at the cutting edge, some are woven entirely from metal thread.

The delight of sheer curtains is that they let the light flood into the room while obscuring the view, so they are the perfect answer when privacy is required. Colored sheers can actually enhance the quality of light entering a room. Blues and greens filter in a clear, fresh light; oranges and reds give warmth; and pinks and yellows give a room a wonderful luminosity that is most welcome on gray and cloudy days.

Opposite page: Perfect for privacy, sheers in a bedroom obscure the view but do not cut out much light. For people who like to wake up naturally with the onset of daylight, they are the perfect solution.

Right: Graceful, emmboidered sheer fabric provides a gentle, chic barrier between the indoors and the garden without blocking the view or the light.

Left: A bridal bed chamber taking full advantage of the romantic possibilities of sheer fabric. The full curtains hang from a slender metal rod with elegant, openwork finials and spill generously onto the floor—a look that works well in a bedroom but should be avoided in rooms with a lot of traffic. Delicate ironwork and gauzy, transparent fabrics go well together, as the ironwork screen placed in front of the window attests.

Center: Machine embroidery on cotton net. This delicate tracery is reminiscent of the crewelwork patterns normally associated with thick wool fabrics. This type of fabric would make wonderful inner curtains or simple pull-up blinds teamed up with heavyweight embroidered outer curtains or dress curtains.

Opposite page: A sheer from the luxury end of the market, this fabric is a hand-embroidered fine silk. Using it at a window with the light diffusing through shows it off beautifully. An effective way of using expensive fabrics is to use a panel set into a generous curtain made from a more budget-conscious complementary fabric; in this case, a solid cream silk would look great as a framework for the exquisite workmanship.

Sheer magic

● Forget the suburban image of old-style net curtains: sheers are the modern decorating phenomenon. New fabric technology means that even the most delicate of fabrics can be treated against sun damage. Many can be easily maintained—and are machine washable.

● Colored sheers enhance the quality of light that enters a room.

● A sheer blind allows you to enjoy the light that comes through the window but obscures the view from the outside. Even delicate sheers can be made up as Roman blinds or roller blinds.

● Embroidered sheers add a subtle, decorative touch that can be reflected in other layers of curtaining.

Simply smart

The smart and tailored look is as much about what to leave out as what to put in. It is about working with the architecture of the room and respecting its horizontal and vertical lines. The result is a space that is calm and beautiful with no frills and little fuss. It is both a modern look and one that is absolutely timeless.

Curtains and blinds are a key element of this look, because the eye is always drawn to the window, where the window treatment sets the tone.

Below: A serene bedroom with wonderful views overlooking the garden. Neat, striped Roman blinds are perfectly fitted inside each sash window, and the fresh green is picked up in the luxurious quilt.

Right: A softly tailored curtain hangs like a standing column at the side of a full-length window. A white venetian blind offers extra privacy and shade if required without intruding on the overall scheme.

No frills

● A modern but timeless decorative scheme looks as good with contemporary furnishings and modern art as it does with antiques and Old Masters.

● This style is not just for modern spaces: rooms with classical proportions and large windows can also benefit from the simple, smart approach.

● Often the simplest solutions are the smartest. Consider this: the purpose of a window is to let in light, not to support yards of intricate drapery.

● The simple style is about form and enjoying the architectural contour of your window.

Simply colorful

If your room needs a big splash of color, the natural place to put it is at the window, because the window is the first thing that catches your eye as you walk in. If you get it right, it will look as stunning as a bold abstract painting.

Left: Silk taffeta curtains in classic blue-and-white stripes add a sense of drama and are perfect for this elegantly proportioned room.

Color, applied simply, can make a very strong statement. If the curtains are to blend in with the walls, the whole room will glow and vibrate with the colorways you have chosen, so you have to be sure you can live with the scheme on a daily basis. Colorful curtains or blinds set into neutral or white walls will become a major feature that cannot be ignored, but there is always the possibility of changing just the curtains, maybe on a seasonal basis, so that winters are welcomed in with warm colors and summers are heralded by a springlike rush of cooler colors.

Left: This stunning fabric has all the pizzazz of deck-chair stripes but is overlaid with white tracery that lifts the straight, simple curtains into the realm of sophistication. The soft red that has been picked out for the wall color is very easy to live with and a perfect foil for decorative antiques.

Right: The view of this sunny garden is framed by a generous curtain in bold, cheerful colors.

CHAPTER THREE

Traditional Style

The formal curtain belongs to the English country house tradition and requires a room of some grandeur if it is to work well. Grand curtains with swags and drapes belong with beautifully proportioned windows—not on picture windows in low-ceilinged, modern homes.

Period homes can suit a variety of curtain styles, from elegant full-length curtains with traditional pleated headings, to an innovative twist on a classic swag.

The full swag and tail

The traditional window treatment has lightened up over the years in keeping with the times. Gone are the dark, light-absorbing velvets and solid damasks with ornate pelmets and stiff gold braids that overpowered windows and obscured light. Today's take on the traditional has all the grace of the past but, thankfully, none of the excess.

A well-designed traditional window treatment should have a timeless feel to it. It should look as if it has always been there, tailor-made for the window and color matched to the room. Swags and tails are synonymous with this type of approach, but they should not be dauntingly formal or stiff. The modern swag is a generous scoop of fabric that hangs in soft pleats, and the tail is a hanging trail of fabric that cascades down the curtain.

Opposite page: This generous treatment has been given a fun touch with heavily-textured edging which emphasizes the swathes of fabric.

Right: A classical asymmetrical arrangement to frame a beautifully proportioned window and a lovely view. The sheer undercurtain is held back with a simple brass rosette, and the yellow silk swag is trimmed with exquisite beaded tassels.

The traditional approach

● For full impact, traditional window treatments need rooms with traditional window shapes and high ceilings.

● Curtains should be generous. Never skimp on the amount of fabric. If cost is an issue, a greater yardage of a cheaper fabric will always win over a scrap of something expensive.

● Traditional curtains need to be beautifully made, and headings and hems should always be hand-sewn.

● Tiebacks give the traditional curtain its style and form. A high tieback lets in more light and gives a modern look; a tieback in the middle is the traditional way; a low tieback lets curtains billow generously.

Elegant simplicity

Even with the rules of traditional window treatments as relaxed as they are, one thing remains paramount: the curtains must be properly made. Good curtains are an investment and should be seen as part of the architecture of the room, not as a throw-away item.

The best curtains are completely hand sewn (apart from the seams joining the widths), which is why they hang so well and never pucker, no matter what fabric is used, and why they are not cheap. The general rule is to allow a minimum of two times the width of the window for each curtain, but most curtain makers opt for two and a half. The ideal length for a full-length curtain is just breaking on the floor.

Right: Generous curtains frame a French window like two pleated columns blending beautifully with the walls.

When choosing fabric for your curtains, consider its texture and weight as much as its color and pattern. There are some truly innovative fabrics available now, and the distinctions have all but disappeared between dress-weight fabrics and furnishing fabrics, apart from the width (furnishing fabrics are made on wider looms). Some of the most exquisite curtains are made from dress-weight beaded lace, silks, and linens, and some of the most dramatic from wool suiting and fake suede.

Before you commit to a fabric, ask for a large returnable sample that you can hang in the window over a pole and observe for a day or two. Fabrics hanging at a window look surprisingly different from small swatches in a sample book.

Left: This antique fabric has a beautiful texture which cannot help but enhance any room.

Opposite page: Exquisitely made dove-gray silk taffeta curtains, meticulously lined and interlined, hang in thick, luxurious folds. They are held in place by a metal arm known as an embrace.

A large mirror maximizes the available light and emphasizes the symmetry of the room.

Blinds set into the frame allow plenty of light into the room and show the windows off to their best advantage.

A lamp and other small objects on the tabletop provide a focal point and help to bring the eye downwards in this lofty room.

Above left: A lovely swoop of unlined fabric makes a stylish room divider. The fabric is simply folded over at the top, then attached with curtain clips to a pole. The fabric is allowed to puddle onto the floor for an opulent look.

Above right: A traditional floral fabric was the inspiration for this bedroom's décor. The cream of the walls and the green of the skirting are colors taken directly from the fabric.

Opposite page: This tailored treatment is formal but still appropriate for a feminine bedroom. The pleated pelmet creates an attractive curve at the top of the window, echoing the shape of the bed frame.

Above left: Light floods into this all-white dining room unimpeded by the simple curtain treatment.

Above right: A symphony of color—a delicate yellow sheer curtain filters warm light into the room, and a blue silk unlined blind provides a dramatic flourish.

Left: A fresh and modern but traditional look features columns both fake and made of fabric. The curtains have interesting smocked headings instead of a pelmet, and they hang in beautiful fluted pleats.

Designers working in the field of classic design are forever looking at new ways of addressing the formal room with new fabrics, new ideas, and a sensitivity toward 21st-century taste with its predeliction for comfort, simplicity, natural light, and less fussy detail.

What is emerging is less heavy velvet and ruffled chintz, a lot more good tailoring, and a pleasing fusion of new ideas with the classics of design. Textured fabrics have come into their own in the form of heavy ribbed silks and diaphanous taffetas. Solid-colored fabrics are more popular now, either decorated with beautiful braids, fringes, tassels, and beads or accented with stripes and checks, and sometimes with occasional interjections of those all-time classic favorites such as chintz and toile de Jouy. Toile depicts idealized 18th-century rural scenes, traditionally in blue or sepia on a white ground. It is named after the French factory near Versailles, where the printing technique was developed.

Opposite page: Here the curtains have been used to unify the different shapes of the windows in this elegant drawing room. The top of the curtains echo the arch of the tallest window and appear to lengthen the proportions of this grand room. Using a muted color prevents the dramatic curtains from dominating the room's design. This stunning treatment is the work of the famous British design company Colefax and Fowler.

Traditional floral

Floral fabrics bring freshness, color, and a touch of romance into a home. The modern approach to florals consists of keeping things simple. Floral curtains look their best either with uncomplicated French pleated headings hung on a pole or with their headings and tracks hidden from view under straightforward pelmets or gathered valances.

Many classic floral patterns are still bestsellers, but the busier, brightly colored florals have given way to more modern, stylized designs inspired by botanical drawings and Oriental flower paintings. An edging of colored braid or solid-colored fabric gives floral curtains a sharper, more modern edge.

When working with large designs, matching up the widths is an important consideration, as is centering the design on pelmets if they are used. Smaller patterns are obviously much easier to work with in this way.

Left: A selection of floral linens and striped tickings, ranging from a stylized modern design to an old-fashioned rose garland pattern.

Opposite page: Pretty in pink. The fresh pink-and-white florals are perfect for an ultrafeminine bedroom. The pattern on the chair is quite bold, while the curtain fabric is more subtle, but the shared colorscheme helps to unite them. The blue walls prevent the pink from overwhelming the room.

Above center: A pretty, old-fashioned design printed on a translucent fabric. The predominance of white gives the curtain a fresh, cottage look that is as appealing as a bouquet of flowers.

Above right: A riot of roses on a sunny yellow ground. The owners have gone all out for this design, matching fabric with wallpaper. In a small room, all-over treatments like this look quaint, rather like a miniature decorated box.

Left: In a light, airy room, delicate, chintzy curtains billow in the wind, creating just the right amount of privacy. The printed fabric echoes the chair and injects a hint of color.

Chintz and beyond

● In a large room, use floral fabrics in moderation. Team them with solid colors.

● Modern floral designs look good teamed with checks and stripes in complementary colors. Use the contrasting fabric as a lining so that you catch glimpses of it as the curtain moves.

● Do not choose complicated pelmet designs. Pick gently gathered valances or fabric-covered pelmet boards.

● Play with the scale of your patterns. Choose big splashy cushion covers in the same colorway. It will give the room a dynamic feel.

● Florals look great in bedrooms.

● Padded and quilted curtains make a room feel cozy and snug.

CHAPTER FOUR

Comfort and Privacy

Bedrooms should be private havens or retreats, with furnishings and curtains working together to create a restful, calm atmosphere. But best of all, the bedroom is a place where you can indulge your decorative fantasies for fairytale bowers or gothic towers.

Bright, light, and white: a teenage girl's pretty bedroom displays a coronet fit for a princess and a light-excluding roller blind.

More than in any other room, window treatments in a bedroom have a job to do—to control light and visibility. Some people are happy to wake with a lightly diffused sunrise, but if you count yourself among those who crave total darkness while sleeping, then you have to start at the window. If you are relying on curtains alone to do the job, they should be lined, and if the windows face the rising sun, they should be lined with a blackout material.

For a lighter, softer look, choose unlined curtains with a blackout roller blind that disappears into the window frame until needed. Light can be diffused and privacy ensured with sheer undercurtains at the window, such as muslin, lace, or silks that gleam seductively in dim light. Heavier outer curtains can come into play when required to block out the morning sun.

Left: A lightweight lace sheer at the window diffuses light into this cream-and-white space. A crisp white lace table cover reinforces the feeling.

Mirrors bounce light around a room. There's plenty of light in this room to bounce, thanks to the lovely sheers at the massive window with its magnificently carved surround.

The mirror is perfectly positioned for privacy. In it you can see the reflection of another window and the way the sheers are hung— with slot headings on a brass pole. These curtains are not meant to be drawn.

The translucent lace spills onto the floor. This looks lovely and relaxed in a bedroom, but you should avoid the puddle effect with heavy curtains because it drags the eye downward.

Sweet dreams

- A bedroom is a relaxing and private space, and the furnishings should reflect this.

- There should be a relationship between the bed and the window treatment because these are the two focal points of the room. The relationship could be as simple as matching trimmings or choosing fabrics for the bed cover and curtains that harmonize but are not identical.

- Bed curtains are a wonderful decorative touch. They can range from the full four-poster treatment to a delicate coronet affixed to the wall behind the bed, supporting a drift of white muslin.

- Bed curtains should relate to window curtains in some way— by reiterating a pelmet detail, for instance.

The total look

There is a lot of fabric in a bedroom—bedding, upholstery, curtains, blinds, to name but a few. It makes sense to coordinate them in some way. For drama, offset a calm, pale palette for walls and windows with a stunning bed cover in a lively shade. To keep the relationship between the elements, you need something as simple as a trim or edging, and the wonderful thing about bed covers is that they are very easy to change.

Total coordination is another route, requiring a dedication to a look or pattern that is not going to fade. If you are going for color, choose classic florals, paisleys, and toiles that have stood the test of time and coordinate beautifully with simple fabrics such as tickings and checks, as well as with solid colors.

Right: A color-coordinated four-poster that comprises a classic toile, a check, white lace, and a pretty floral quilt. Blue and white is classic colorway that is easy to live with, being neither particularly feminine nor masculine.

Far right: Full-length curtains dress the windows in a grandly proportioned bedroom. Touches of matching fabric have been used judiciously on an armchair and a lampshade.

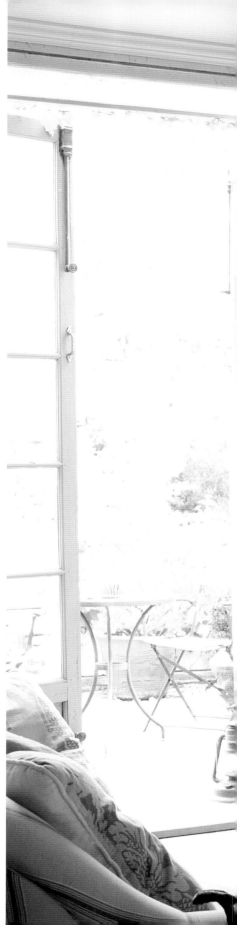

All-over treatments, with one pattern overlaid on another pattern, require a deft hand and a discerning eye. The treatment can be stunning, but it is one of the hardest looks to achieve because you have to balance and judge not only the color but also the scale of the patterns and their style. Finding just the right type of check to give an edge to a dramatic floral is not a job for an amateur.

If a bed laden with rich fabrics is to be the main focal point, then give it the space it deserves to be admired, and choose muted colors and patterns that are not too dense for the walls and window curtains. If the various elements in a room have to fight for attention, there are no winners.

Using the same pattern for all fabric, wallpaper, and bed coverings is a bold decision and rarely a total success unless the scheme is liberally interspersed with solid color. A bedroom that is too busy is not a relaxing place to be.

Opposite page: Using fabrics and wallpapers printed with traditional patterns makes a room feel comfortable and familiar. The all-over patterns on the walls and ceiling of this attic bedroom are cleverly contrasted with plain curtains and naked bedposts.

Right: A corner of the same room shows how well the various patterns go together, and how their impact is doubled thanks to the simple curtain treatment and the smart, white woodwork.

Match and match

● Uncomplicated curtain treatments look best with bold patterns and traditional fabrics.

● Prints of different scales in the same colorways look good together.

● Dark bed curtains can feel oppressive. Lining them with white fabric will give a fresher, lighter feeling.

● Large, repeated patterns must be carefully handled and well matched. Always make sure to buy sufficient wallpaper and/or fabric from the same batch, as color variations can occur.

● For a masculine all-over pattern, use strongly colored stripes, checks, and plaids instead of florals and lace.

Opposite page: Prettily pink but not overwhelmingly so. This is a delicate decorative scheme, inspired by the elegant lines of antique furniture.

Right: A paneled and beamed bedroom with a quantity of dark, gleaming wood gets a dose of freshness in the form of a delicate brass four-poster bed bedecked with blue and white linens and lace.

Pastel colors teamed up with white are restful and refreshing. For a feminine color scheme, pink and white is the obvious choice, although pink comes in many shades, from coral to shocking, and the effect is not always fairytale bower. Yellows, greens, and blues can be styled in either a masculine or feminine way and are a good choice for a shared bedroom.

Just as there are many shades of blue, from sea-spray gray to cornflower, there are as many shades of white. When choosing a white fabric for curtains or a white paint for walls, consider that the light coming into the room will be affected not only by texture but also by shade: brilliant white dazzles, creamy colors gleam.

Left: A tentlike feeling has been created in this bold bedroom by using pleated fabric attached to the walls on battens. When drawn, the matching curtains complete the illusion. The white bed linen acts as a foil and a go-between for the confidently striped walls and the vibrant, checked bed cover.

Opposite page: Wall and curtain treatments in warm neutral colors give this bedroom a really cozy feel. Bed curtains in the same fabric complete the look.

A small country-farmhouse bedroom with romantically distressed plaster walls is the perfect place for an afternoon siesta. To soften the strong lines of the window, a length of pretty braided fringing is tacked onto the top edge.

The deep recess frames the window, making it as important as an Old Master painting on the wall. A pull-down blind keeps out moonlight and sunlight when required.

Paintwork and plasterwork are gently distressed, giving the room a timeless feel.

The color palette is restricted to gray and white. The quilted bed cover and extravagant pillows give the room a necessary dose of comfort and warmth.

Left: Patterns and solid colors work wonderfully well together. The warm, red walls are the cue for the gray-and-red print curtains, the ornate upholstered chair, and the jaunty gingham-check lampshade. Note how the headboard and the valance around the mattress match the curtains for a nice throw-away touch.

Opposite page: A room within a room, made possible only because the bedroom in question is enormous. A floor-to-ceiling enclosure around the bed has curtains of its own. Inner lining curtains are warmly colored and softly pleated in contrast to the strong shape of the outer structure.

Left: A pretty but spare bedroom with a lovely, fresh, country feel. Full-length lace curtains give the cottage windows a long, lean look, and wooden colonial shutters control light and privacy. Faded tapestries and lace make a stylish and romantic bedroom combination.

Right: Choosing patterns that work together is no hit-or-miss affair. Here, there is a lovely mix of scales, styles, and textures; what unites them is a fresh informality.

Mix and match

● For an all-over treatment with a lighter look, mix solid colors with patterned fabric and keep furnishings and clutter to a minimum.

● Wooden floors and iron bedsteads instantly give a bedroom a country feeling.

● A pillowcase or cushion cover in the same fabric as the bedroom curtains provides a unifying touch.

● With floral fabric around the windows and matching wallpaper on the walls, an all-white bed is an oasis of calm.

● Curtains give a bathroom a luxurious feel and add a touch of drama. Choose a simple style and a fabric that can tolerate a bit of steam and damp.

CHAPTER FIVE

Close-up on Curtains

It is in the detailing of curtains that creativity and craftsmanship really show. Beautiful trimmings and an elegant pole can turn a plain piece of fabric into something very special, and a wonderful lace blind can transform a window into a work of art.

A cheerful voile lets the sun shine in. Sheers look best with simple headings like the loop heading, above.

Poles and finials

Poles have personalities of their own, so it is important to match your pole to your curtain treatment. There are plenty to choose from these days—from the rustic tree branch or length of bamboo to a pole of fluted brass. Poles do a magnificent job behind the scenes—there are poles made of plastic that are literally invisible and, at the other end of the scale, exuberant twists of filigree metal that are designed to be admired.

Today, interior designers are not just consulting conventional catalogs for ideas on curtain-hanging systems, they are also hunting for new ideas at marine suppliers—stainless-steel wire and sail cleats, for instance. Minimalist, cutting-edge designers are using industrial fittings that were never intended for domestic use.

Above: An unusual scalloped and pleated pelmet tied to a simple pole heads up a curtain treatment in a classic toile de Jouy fabric, giving tradition a modern twist.

Opposite page: A bed that demands attention. The coronet from which these graceful bed curtains hang is beautifully decorated with ornate leaves that complement the light fitting.

Curtains can be attached directly to poles in a variety of ways. The simplest fixture is the slot heading—literally a slot at the top of a curtain for the pole to pass through. However, method is not particularly efficient if you want to draw the curtains rather than just tie them back. Tie headings and loop headings will allow the curtains to move more easily; if ease of movement is particularly important to you, choose metal poles rather than wooden ones, which tend to stick.

Above: Beautiful examples of ironwork finials. The stylized wrought-iron fleur-de-lis is a lovely interpretation of a classic. The openwork metal ball has a light, modern look.

Above: Checkered voile curtains with headings tied in smart, chunky bows. The carved-leaf finial is bold and makes an arresting shape against the plain white wall.

Finials finish off a pole with a wonderful flourish, as well as doing the rather mundane job of stopping the curtains from falling off the end. They come in an enormous variety of styles, from simple wooden balls and metal *fleurs-de-lis* to carved animals' heads and clusters of seashells, and they offer a golden opportunity to add a touch of wit and whimsy to an interior. An important or eye-catching finial draws the eye up to the top the curtains, adding interest and apparent height to the room.

Curtain headings and valances

Whether or not to use pelmets and valances is a style choice. On the plus side, they make tall windows more intimate and grand curtain treatments grander, and they hide a multitude of sins in the form of brackets and tracks. On the minus side, they cut out a lot of light and, if you are using a patterned fabric, require a lot of juggling to get the right elements in the right place.

Pelmets are usually made of wood or a stiffening fabric such as buckram, which is then covered in fabric. The pelmet board is fitted above the window and extends beyond it on either side to accommodate drawn curtains.

Valances are made of fabric that has been gathered, ruched, or pleated into headings similar to curtain headings. They create a softer effect than pelmets.

Proportions are important. As a rough guide, the drop of a pelmet or valance should never exceed one-sixth of the total drop of the curtains.

A breezy bedroom decorated in a classic toile de Jouy. A pretty cut-out pelmet crowns the top of the sash window.

This small window would have been overpowered by a curtain. A neat white roller blind provides privacy and controls light, while the unusual pelmet keeps the link between wall and window treatments.

Whether as fabric or wallpaper, classic toile de Jouy is a perennial favorite that transcends fashion.

Headings

● Use the simplest form of curtain heading possible. The traditional French pleat heading, in which pleats are hand sewn in groups of three with flat areas between them, suits practically every style from the grand sweep to the informal hook, ring, and pole.

● Gathered headings are best used for lightweight fabrics or sheers. They are not recommended for long, weighty curtains.

● Pencil pleats are formed by narrow folds that, to work well, should be done by hand. They are best on plain fabrics but look busy with patterns.

● Goblet pleats (pleats the shape of wine glasses), stiffened or stuffed with Dacron, are very dramatic. They are best for fixed dress curtains, since it is difficult to draw them back without bunching.

● Smocked headings need careful sewing. They are good for displaying solid colors or simple stripes.

● Slot headings conceal all but the finials of the pole threaded through.

● Looped or tie headings are used for informal curtains hanging from a simple pole.

Above: Jaunty tasseled pennants take their inspiration from the yellow of the walls rather than from the blue-and-white patterned curtains.

Right: Looped headings on a sheer curtain. With every doubling of the fabric, the color intensifies.

Below: Simple rings complement a classic tailored heading.

Opposite page: Sheer inner curtains are gathered onto a narrow pole using slot headings. Outer dress curtains of heavy cotton damask are loop-headed onto a wooden pole.

Beautiful proportions need little in the way of dressing up. Seen through an archway, a large French window opens wide onto the garden.

A thickly padded, scalloped pelmet is affixed to the ceiling on a narrow, gilded cornice. The pelmet clears the top of the French windows so that the doors open easily and no light is lost.

Lined silk curtains hang straight down from the decorative pelmet, ensuring that the pelmet is the focal point of this luxuriously restrained, neutral-colored room.

Drawing attention to the glorious sweep of this arch, dramatic door curtains are threaded onto a curved pole decorated with carved wooden leaves painted white.

The curtains are gathered into metal embraces—hooks that hold the curtains back—as there is no question of drawing them apart. A low tieback gives the curtain extra fullness.

The curtains are cut generously to spill onto the floor, and well-lined and interlined so that they hang heavy and full. They hold all the drama and promise of theater curtains.

A soft flowing swath of fabric at a window is very appealing—it is the best possible place to showcase a beautiful fabric—so it is not surprising that swag draperies and tails were once so popular. There are, however, plenty of modern solutions that give you the effect of loose drapes without dragging your home back into the Colonial era.

The simplest way of all is to throw fabric over a pole, using a length measuring little more than twice the drop of the window so that both ends bunch at floor level. You can then pull back the front piece, leaving the rear section to hang loose, or tie it back at the same or a different level. This arrangement works particularly well with fine, translucent fabrics because it does tend to obscure the window.

Another simple way to give your curtains a bit of a swagger is to incorporate a shawl valance, which is nothing more than a long frill that flops over the top of the curtain headings, making an instant, stylish valance that lets in light. Line your curtains with something surprising and enjoy the effect as the lining material surfaces as the valance.

Opposite page: Soft top. A gently knotted piece of plaid silk taffeta adds interest and a bit of edge to these abundant sugar-pink curtains.

Right: Curtains of ruched parachute silk cascade like waterfalls from these tall windows. The curtains are held back with café clips and threaded onto simple poles.

Tiebacks and trims

Although the modern preference is for curtains to hang straight down, like pillars of fabric on either side of the window, tiebacks do give the more traditional style curtains a great sense of drama. They create interesting trailing effects at the hem and can be positioned to show off interesting glimpses of a contrasting lining or a tantalizing undercurtain.

Tiebacks can be as simple or as elaborate as the curtain demands. For traditional styles, choose from silk ropes and tassels, plaited and padded tiebacks, or shaped tiebacks made from stiffened fabric. For the more modern look, there is an amazing array of curtain trimmings crafted in all manner of materials, including ethnic jewelry, leather, seashells, and ceramic beads. In the relentless search for the new, manufacturers are going back to old pattern books and using wonderful materials like feathers and crystal droplets that have not been seen near curtains since the 18th century.

Opposite page: The ultimate tieback—a luscious, handmade silk tassel, color-coordinated with the fabric.

Right: A novel approach. Curtains made from the finest parachute silk are tucked behind an empty oval mirror frame. The solid shape of the frame contrasts with the diaphanous nature of the curtains.

Window jewelry

● Think of trimmings as adding jewelry and makeup to your curtains.

● Heavy, lined, and interlined traditional curtains will need tiebacks that are as visually forceful as the curtains themselves: Think big beautiful tassels and thick silk rope.

● Tie back flower-sprigged muslins and cottons with tiny bunches of silk flowers and raffia.

● Glass beads make wonderful curtain trimmings: they play with the light, sparkle like diamonds, and make a wonderful sound like wind chimes in the breeze.

● To outline the shape of a curtain, trim the leading edge and hem with a textured braid or bobble edging. If you use a trim in the same color as the curtain fabric, the effect will be subtle but effective.

● Beads, ethnic jewelry, and seashells make unusual trims. Use them to edge pelmets and valances, too.

● Show off contrasting linings and undercurtains by pulling the top layer back. If you do not want to see the tieback, use a metal swing arm, known as an embrace, which is affixed to the wall beside the curtain.

Opposite page: Bobble-trimmed curtains embracing a breakfast corner are held in place with matching trimmed tiebacks to reveal an enticing border of lining material.

Right: Simple cord tiebacks at a high level give these curtains a very classical look rather like a pair of fluted columns with an exuberant pediment.

Opposite page: A bobble trim with an enchanting difference. The bobbles hang from the edge of this blind like berries for the birds.

Above: Simple tie-on sheers frame a bedroom window that has been dressed with delicate gold-colored butterflies hanging from the frame. Dressing the window can be about more than the curtains or blinds themselves.

Embroidery and old lace

● "I hope it is not necessary for me to go into the matter of lace curtains here. I feel sure that no woman of really good taste could prefer a cheap curtain of imitation lace to a simple one of white muslin." —*Elsie de Wolfe, 1910*

● The strict definition of lace is a fabric created not by weaving but by construction with either a needle or bobbins.

● Today's embroidered sheers and machine-made laces are delicate, attractive, and affordable. They look wonderful at windows where the light plays through the patterns.

● The chief use of lace and embroidery in curtain treatments is in trimmings and borders, or for larger pieces, as undercurtains or blinds.

Blinds and shutters

Like curtains, blinds and shutters help control heat and light, dampen noise, and provide privacy. They also offer practical solutions for awkward windows and an alternative where curtains would be inappropriate.

Blinds are less overpowering than curtains, because they allow the architecture of the window to remain uncluttered. But it is important to get the proportions right: Blinds should be longer than they are wide. If you have a wide window, hang several narrow blinds rather than one wide one. This will give you the flexibility you need to control light and have a softening effect on a large expanse of glass.

Above: Roman blinds sit neatly within the elegant frames, dressing the windows without dominating them.

Right: A light room with an airy Colonial feel, appropriately furnished with iron chaises and palms in pots and decorated in shades of white. Curtains would be out of place here. Each pair of tall French windows has two narrow pull-up blinds fitted neatly within the glazing bars to control light and to shade the room from the sun. Antique, lime-washed external shutters flank the room as decorative elements, adding to the cool, breezy atmosphere.

Above left: A cane roll-up blind on the window of a lovely, lacy bedroom. Cane blinds do not keep out a lot of light, but the light will be very mellow.

Above right: A neat, striped Roman blind. Roman blinds look good on their own because they fold into neat pleats, like a pelmet.

Facing page: The embroidery on this Roman blind echoes the view of the garden beyond.

Wooden blinds and shutters give a room atmosphere—the sunlight that streams through has a warm, mellow feel. Wooden Venetian blinds have an architectural quality that gives faceless windows definition, although they do require a lot of space to stack at the top. Colonial shutters with adjustable louvers need space to stack at the sides of windows when they are not in use. Their big plus, apart from their good looks, is in the small adjustable panels that leave you in total control of light and privacy.

Cane and bamboo blinds are inexpensive and stylish and look good alongside casual furnishings. That said, you can find antique Japanese bamboo blinds edged with silk ribbon that would look as good at the window of an elegant traditional home as in an expensively decorated, minimalist apartment.

Above: Here, a striped blind with elegant, tailored folds brings a masculine touch to the room, but the look is softened by the generous swag of curtain framing the daybed area.

Fabric blinds offer a wonderful opportunity to showcase a lovely textile. Your room will suggest a type of fabric to use, and the look you want from the fabric—neat and tailored or softly ruched—will suggest a blind treatment. Roman blinds stack into neat pleats when pulled up and look like a tailored panel of fabric when down. Stripes and solid colors look good as Roman blinds, which are best when lined, as this improves the way the pleats fall.

Roller blinds have been around since the 18th century. They have a neat, tailored look and can be made from just about any fabric, from soft sheers for elegant drawing rooms to waterproof sail cloth for kitchens and bathrooms. With the addition of tracks at the side, the mechanism can be adapted so blinds

pull up from the bottom, obscuring the lower half of the window for privacy while letting light in at

the top. These versatile blinds can also be adapted for sloping windows.

Festoon blinds are usually made of an unlined fabric. They hang straight when let down, but balloon

into pleated folds when drawn up by cords that run through looped tape or rings sewn onto the back.

The number of cords dictates the number of balloons, and the stiffness of the fabric the nature of the

folds. If they are decorated with too many frills and trims they can be overly ornate and lavish and risk

looking decidedly old-fashioned. The answer is to keep them simple, without too much yardage, so you

can enjoy the effect of soft folds of fabric catching the light.

Left: A series of plain white Roman blinds has been skillfully tailored to fit this massive wall of windows. Each blind fits neatly within one element, enabling the occupants to control the amount of light entering the room.

Facing page: A simple white roller blind provides privacy and shelter from the sun, without cluttering the elegant lines of the full-height window.

Left: Roman blinds made from sheer white organza, with wide stripes of pale taupe at either side. This is the minimalist way to decorate with blinds—no frills or trims, just perfect craftsmanship and a restrained color palette.

Index

Picture Credits

All photographs © Hearst Books except those that appear on the following pages:

p8 © Fritz von der Schulenburg—The Interior Archive (Designer: Mimmi O'Connell)
p16 © Fritz von der Schulenburg—The Interior Archive (Designer: Richard Hudson)
p26 © Fritz von der Schulenburg—The Interior Archive (Designer: Colefax & Fowler)
p31 © Fritz von der Schulenburg—The Interior Archive
p88 © Fritz von der Schulenburg—The Interior Archive (Designer: Colefax & Fowler)
p115 © Fritz von der Schulenburg—The Interior Archive (Designer: Jerry Welling)
p150 © Fritz von der Schulenburg—The Interior Archive

ACKNOWLEDGMENTS

This has been a real team effort and the author would like to thank Christine Wood, Corinne Asghar and everyone at Cico Books for their help and support.

The publishers would like to thank Alison Wormleighton for editorial help.